Little Book of Sociology

Little Book of Sociology

An Intelligence Officer's Viewpoint

By
Mohammed M. Hunafa

E-BookTime, LLC
Montgomery, Alabama

Little Book of Sociology
An Intelligence Officer's Viewpoint

ISBN: 978-1-60862-582-6

First Edition
Published December 2014
E-BookTime, LLC
6598 Pumpkin Road
Montgomery, AL 36108
www.e-booktime.com

Contents

Introduction

From the very beginning of history sociology of the world has been the intricate attempt of man and civilization to get the totality of what the world should be right with itself for the sake of mankind's objectivity. Essentially, what the initial instance was were that man existed from the beginning in a state of primordial inconclusiveness. He was in essence an animalistic and indeterminate bundle of ignorance. Further, as man started first to collect himself in his first duty to himself and his associates was the forming of his psychology and later his sociology. This on the surface may seem to have been a rather routine task, but as man in the beginning was unprepared for this venture he was, if one goes by what history has been, a complete and abysmal amateur at this job. A lot can be said about why man did so poorly at integrating himself holistically with that of the designs he had for his society and why even in today's time he still has not done a complete job of the work that was so important. For, by this time, man could be in the utopia of worlds he had yet to design.

In this book I will take you through stages from the beginning to the current time of man's journey throughout his life singularly and collectively as it came to represent his attempts to globalize the world even before we knew that was what man was attempting. In this book the United States Security/Police Agency will act as mechanical instrumentation that provides the truth about the subject in question.

Since its beginning in 2011 the Agency has accepted the duty of being the one source of truth the people can count on for the unquestionable knowledge every human needs to know about subjects never before touched on by any other source to date. The

United States Security/Police Agency, in order to do its job, has become one with all origins of intelligence in the world. We at the Agency are what in the intelligence community are what one might understand as being "tapped in" to the very places in which intelligence the world over originates. We, in addition to specializing in terms of intelligence, make our product to the consumer succinct and enjoyable to read with the end product cooperative to the diverse readership we hope to touch with our writings.

This little book on the history of sociology will touch not only man's beginning and where he has progressed to, but what, where, and why the job he has done is not yet as complete as it should be. So without restricting you from the knowledge on this subject any longer, let's jump right into our story. I should also say that as Director of the U.S. Security/Police Agency the pledge I make in all my books is to be the best source of truth and knowledge available today that the people have. That is my committed, undying service.

Mohammed M. Hunafa
Director of the U.S. Security/Police Agency

Chapter 1

Primordial Ineffectiveness and Formalism

We start off with the individual capacity of man's design for himself psychologically and progress to the sociological aspects of life. Firstly, before man had for himself the dominating nature for his society he had the individual task of getting for himself the ordering of his psychology. That was an awesome undertaking for, in the first instance, man was not man as he should have been to do the job the right way from the very beginning. Man in all that he was at best improperly orientated and was in need of grasping what the universe, himself, and his world should be in which he existed as an impediment. He was of course as can be attributed to in knowing his history without the correct formulation of what a psychology is and should be to do the great job of ordering his society.

Even before the great question of the societal design he had deep within himself was to play out on the scenes of this world, man did not first have a grasp of what it entailed to complete the process. So of course he floundered. Eons have passed since that first beginning to date and we as a world in process are still struggling as the first man did to order his society. Like I said, he had himself to order first. The truth of this world indicated in man and his society was to know self first.

His journey as it was then begins now with the first man in mind and modern day man as he has progressed. It is in true understanding of the problem that the following is stated. Man as he was in the first instance and the man he is today has changed little, taken as an equilateral equation, shared so much yet improved so little. Both aspects of man in total output in the world since the beginning suffered the objective of progress to the point that each man (the past one and the future one) have displayed only a small element of domination of the world for good. Both aspects of man as it relates to the collective whole of man in what genius he depicted in the world both psychologically and sociologically did in fact never attain the true sociological dominance the world would have him be, to be truly the ruler of the free world. I mean this. Man, past and present and collectively as a species, still exists without ever having developed the most perfect sociology. That is a true and definite fact.

Wherever you look throughout the world there is still need for improvement. It was the destiny of each man in the whole of the world to do sociologically in one lifetime what was the true order for society to be great and problem free. Individually and collectively we have not yet accomplished that feat. The $100,000 question is to honestly ask yourself, "Have we the best of sociological molds that can be attained?" The truth is, without blaming someone else who may or may not be a real sociologist, it seems that for a lack of ability the field of sociology is wanting in the form of those sociologists that can alleviate the turmoil we live with today as true sociologists.

Chapter 2

The Dark Ages, Middle Ages, and Industrialized Ages

As it pertains to the Dark Ages and ancient man of that period with special reference to the overall approach necessary for sound psychology and ultimately sociology – man was termed to be a factor of his own misunderstanding of his psychology and his sociology. The evolution of man began from the first instance of his existence. He was essentially steeped in a cosmos of the unknown and chaos that displayed itself in how he was not knowledgeable in consideration of his own survival. It was his survival and ultimately the domination of his society that was the goal.

The evolution and the actual representation of life man historically lived as we would come to realize was inconsistent and degrading on the scale of which survival could be his. His shelters were haphazard and stemmed from an innate inability to structure shelters that guarded him from the elements and wild animals. His food was at times not nutritional and bland. There were no stoves of electricity he was responsible for creating. This was the essence of the Dark Ages as it had reflection on the ill-equipped ability of man to adequately provide for himself and his structure. The overall implication is that what man created with sense would have had then and now is that which took him eons to achieve was at his discretion then.

The point I am trying to make is this. What has taken him eons to reach in his design with respect to himself and his society was and is the mystery of the development of his psychology. The necessary smarts to bypass the needed cultivation of himself and his design for sociology mysteriously has never been right to do the job right, then or now. You might say that isn't true, but if one knows that even the slightest medical, administrational, or mechanical feat of genius was something it took him eons to accomplish and even today the things he has created often at first seem practical we often times see him going back to the "drawing board" and reworking his initial project. This is where man then and now is flawed.

What is needed before I get into the description of the Middle Ages is precognition. I mean here an innate knowledge of the totality of earth domination, a strategy that when one moves the first chess piece on the board of life he already knows his last chess move. Whatever you might term this state, it is the direct reason man is not the dominate force his accomplishments would have us believe. On some oh so subtle scale precognition of everything before it is everything must be fully contemplated and known. A term I have deemed "spatial realization" seems to be missing in man's psychology and sociology. That has been the primary reason on a grand scale that man and his society has flaws, even by today's standards.

Continuing his legacy without the correction of his spatial realization, I move on to give you a depiction of actions that have flowed from the very first instance of not having the proper spatial realization that in fact was missing with regard to man and his accomplishments and what if he had spatial realization from the start and how he would have avoided making society in a way that has left us with obvious holes in it. Had man perhaps been empowered with the power of spatial realization we might have a cure for AIDS or cancer.

The Middle Ages brought into existence the legacy man had laid out for his history in the fact that the Dark Ages was without the forces of spatial realization and precognition; a period where man first established the misordering of his psychology and ultimately his sociology. As was stated, the Dark Ages as a set descriptive of the faculties of reason man lacked was the starting mechanics of rationalization that from that point would forever produce an irresolution of the world in terms of correct order that man so needed to get things right.

The Middle Ages produced a concomitant pact of nation states all establishing themselves energetically to conquer other nations and colonial aspirations that propped up their own societies at the disadvantage of others. Wars were the central theme and with states like England, Rome, Greece, and Arabia vying for control and power throughout the then known world, the earth itself became a hotbed of anti-sociological objectives that brought about degradation to most of the conquered states of the time. The Crusades were a factor in establishing the misnomer of war as the only means that one state used on another to survive. If you remember earlier in this book survival and a reckless survival was the norm. Inept performances of the psychological discipline made man into little more than a savage beast devastating everything in his wake as he laid desolate hundreds and even thousands of nations. England, the only known surviving nation from the Middle Ages with its kings and queens established on the thrown, fostered some civilization during the period, but even still, their maniacal desire to own and have more consistent with other monarchies of the time in the name of exploration continued to wreak havoc on the then known world. This was surely not the type of sociology that the world needed but nevertheless was the line of travel into history man had made for himself.

The Middle Ages saw power and control throughout Europe change hands many times as nation states committed themselves to war at all cost and it was not until Europe set its eyes on the westward expansion of their strongholds in Europe did we really get a taste for the bloodthirsty nature of man to conquer everything in his wake at all cost. In the new world called America the savagery that the Europeans brought to this new land saw the nation exploited for its then known wealth to bring more and more power to the monarchies of Europe. Then the foundling nation called America sought to establish itself as an independent nation and with that establishment more devastation and decadence was to follow.

Next we talk about the Industrialized Age. Whatever else you may take away from what you have read so far in this book, you know the sociology that was followed was not sound sociology. It was a sociology we find common throughout the world even today were the line of travel has been one where we still are fighting wars, people throughout the world go without nutritional food, and the rich get richer and the poor stay poor.

From the pre-industrialization era leading up through the industrialization era in America, throughout the history to include the country's conception through to the 21st century, we have a list of sociological patterns that speak to the typology of sociology the world practiced then and now. Mind you this is not the sociology of textbooks written by austere minds holding PhD's but the type that makes for destruction and chaos the world over. Here is the list:

- The break away from England and the Revolutionary War

- The displacement and subjugation of the Native American Indians that lasted up to and throughout the Civil War

- The enslavement of the people from Africa

- The Civil War that saw hundreds of thousands killed on both sides of Americans fighting this war

- The industrialization of America that brought about steam powered transportation and factories with the devastation of the air, rivers and lakes from pollutants

- Suffrage for women and blacks in terms of labor and voting rights

- Automobiles, trains, and planes that contributed to more pollution

- World War I

- World War II and the creation of atomic weapons including hydrogen bombs

- The Korean War

- The War in Vietnam

- The conflict in Somalia

- Two Iraq Wars

- The War in Afghanistan

- Ultimately the War on Terrorism that is still with us today.

These are some of the major points in the history of this country that have actions that contributed to an insanity in sociology from both the micro and macro approaches to sociology. Had we known way back when in our first instance of development the question remains if we would have laid out a history for ourselves that would have produced the catastrophes the world has experienced up to today's time. This form of sociology is, like I said, different than a sociology that fosters wellness, health and progress for the people of this country. With so much desolation during this history it is a wonder we would term what we have produced sociology.

In the next chapter I will deal with sociology from the standpoint of when it is done right like right minded practitioners have done and when it is done the way history has recorded. I will also deal with micro and macro sociology to better give a picture how all facets of a good sociology works for progress and innovation in this country.

Chapter 3

History of American Sociology

When people think of American sociology what usually comes to mind are big scientific and/or technological breakthroughs in social design normally undertaken by governmental agencies that are committed to the revolutionizing of the American social structure.

What also goes along with that depiction is the ever so real aspect of big governmental intervention in society which is also called macro-sociology that works from the big picture perspective of life in this country that deals with issues like health care, criminal justice and the courts, the workforce, the welfare state, and social life in general. This macro approach in sociology thinks the grander perspective from a top down formula works best, at least from the vantage point of top notch sociologists, so that in their planning they at the very top include all sectors of the populous to make it easier from the perspective of everyday Americans to objectively be touched in their lives from a micro perspective. It goes without saying that these macro-sociologists take into consideration when planning the micro perspective of everyday ordinary Americans that life in general is made easier but in most cases they fail.

With the ever present and surging rates of crime and unemployment little help is the reality the macro-sociologists offer. Many would say the problems are and have gotten too big and out of hand to control now. Then there are those that know of what I spoke of in the earlier chapters in the book refer-encing the course of history where catas-trophe was the rule of the day and the magnification and deepening of the problems made it even more difficult to handle these problems even at today's standards. Macro-sociologists then without a righteous path to follow have thrown in the towel and done the most prudent job they could. That itself is the failing of the ages as we move through history. The question then is will we ever get control again?

The micro approach to the elderly who worked their entire lives to only find in retirement an insufficient social security system that little affords them an existence is the reality. That the youth of this country remain faced with a school drop out rate that is too high and early teen parenting not to mention sometimes drugs and alcohol is a problem. There are even trends that continue from the sixties and seventies of broken and abusive home life which is a problem. Many who are fortunate enough to find themselves in college are negative on the aspect of finding suitable employment when they graduate. Homelessness is pervasive and life in the country at best is dismal for a great many Americans.

Where would we be if the sociologists had gotten the job right at first? The following is a list of what correct sociology would have addressed by now in this country and even a thought of whether the issues listed would ever have been problems in the first place:

- Immigration would not be a problem

- Unemployment would be nonexistent

- Homelessness would be eradicated

- Gay and lesbian right to marry would be a fact

- Gun control would not be a problem

- Racial profiling by police would not exist

- Justice Department surveillance of Americans for possible terrorist activity would not exist

These are just a few of the questions that good sociologists would have answered. This is not to provide us with a totally black picture that sociologists in the country have gone over to a dark practice of sociology, but it sure seems that way. Whether dealing with the sociologists and the macro approach, or the average American and the micro approach, what was needed was a prospect of handling the sociological problem from the standpoint of a modern day miracle worker. As I just proposed, there might be some truth to what some think that there is a government conspiracy with sociology in mind. I will address that notion in the next chapter.

Chapter 4

The Great Game

Since sociology has taken a dark turn in the world from its inception, some have gone as far as to claim there is a conspiracy of the world's most powerful governments.

A new term "The Great Game" is and was the description of the rivalry and conflict between the British Empire and the Russian Empire for supremacy in Central Asia from the period 1813 - 1917. Arthur Connoly, a British intelligence officer of the East India Company coined the term describing intelligence efforts of the time. The Great Game is a New Age descriptive accepted by all major players in geopolitical aspirations around the world of which the intelligence/security services have taken up the mantle of what was started at the beginning of civilized society in the form of skewed sociology that replaced good actions with bad ones. Having no recourse other than the skewed path that status quo sociology took, the efforts of those that were sociologists became the playground of police agencies, the court and social services systems and the world's intelligence agencies.

This new game fell in line with the inadequate path that had been laid by early sociologists and took off in the form of sociology that was the field of intelligence and the intelligence services that ran the programs. The major players with the advent of the intelligence and whether in the real sociology was just the acts of these major players in hidden intelligence and the programs that went along with this innovative field. If one knows anything about the field of intelligence, especially when sociology is taken as part of intelligence functions, we get a better representation of what the world is trying to accomplish. Often in covert and clandestine means and methods the world's major players wield awesome power in regulating their own nations, not to mention competing nations involving themselves in intelligence pursuits. If taken in this frame and with appreciation of the fact sociology, like intelligence, is a formidable set of activities we then know where the world is now headed. With what has just been said and the covert and clandestine methods used to secure their own futures the Great Game will be such well into the future.

Chapter 5

Endgame Provisions

Needless to say that if in fact the world has traded in conventional sociology for that of the intelligence program we then can see of whence we came. If covert and clandestine means to solve the world's problems is left up to intelligence we know, based on what intelligence has historically been, most of what we can expect will be carried out in ways that remain secret to most of the populous of the world. Only those operating within the boundaries of intelligence will be the knowledge holders of these secret programs. What this means for our future is that the future is not secure.

We have less involvement with activity when intelligence is in use than there might have ever been a man on the moon. What we can be sure of is intelligence is one of the two oldest professions. With that reality we can be sure of one thing, the wars and the displaced societies of the world will continue. Intelligence of the type that has been the custom in the world that we know offers us the concept that nothing about the real solutions we need will ever come into existence. The contentious methods that have been the earmark of intelligence services throughout the world are really what we don't need. The powers that be; however, have determined differently and what we can again be sure of is that intelligence, whether of the devil or God, is an institution that is here to stay. This is the complete picture of American sociology as it exists today.

Chapter 6

Conclusion

As an intelligence service with the right frame of reference about the profession of intelligence it was an exciting undertaking to write this book for you. If nothing more is ever known of the secretive intelligence services of the world, rest assured this intelligence service will always follow an open disclosure policy, hence this book. The world of intelligence, as was said, is a tremendous undertaking and one that carries with it an immense responsibility. With the vast sources at our disposal, unlike other intelligence sources, we will always pledge to the American people to provide an honest and forthright intelligence product and it is our pleasure to do so.

In a world where little is known of what occurs in the field of intelligence, we at this agency will remain committed to not only an approach to intelligence that is without secrets we will remain devoted to the true approach to implementing the right type of sociology for this country's betterment. Hence the second reason for this book. After all is said and done, this agency will always stand as a beacon of hope for a future that is progressive to all that may depend on our efforts. Never will we at the agency betray your trust.

Yours truly,

Mohammed M. Hunafa
Director of the U.S. Security/Police Agency

www.ingramcontent.com/pod-product-compliance
Lightning Source LLC
Chambersburg PA
CBHW061932280526
45787CB00004B/1578